John A. McCabe

Legal Disclaimers

This report is presented to you for informational purposes only and is not a substitution for any professional advice. The contents herein are based on the views and opinions of the author and all associated contributors.

While every effort has been made by the author and all associated contributors to present accurate and up to date information within this document, it is apparent guidelines, rules and laws change. Therefore, the author and all associated contributors reserve the right to update the contents and information provided herein as these changes progress. The author and/or all associated contributors take no responsibility for any errors or omissions if such discrepancies exist within this document.

The author and all other contributors accept no responsibility for any consequential actions taken, whether monetary, legal, or otherwise, by any and all readers of the materials provided. It is the reader's sole responsibility to seek professional advice before taking any action on their part.

Readers results will vary based on their skill level and individual perception of the contents herein, and thus no guarantees, monetarily or otherwise, can be made accurately. Therefore, no guarantees are made.

About This Book

Every once in a while a revolutionary idea, system or model comes along that completely transforms the landscape of an industry.

This book is not your traditional real estate investing book, but rather answers the two questions I have been getting since 2009 from hundreds of real estate investors just like you. First, "How did you find that lead or opportunity?" and second, "How did you do that deal with no money, credit or partners?"

My guess is you're here right now because you have a mission, a purpose, and a desire for a lifestyle change, control over what you do and how you do it. You're here because you want more money. Maybe you want to quit your job, create passive income and control real estate, and maybe you're just getting started....

I know what that feels like. It's why my passion has been to help people get unstuck from the real estate investing quicksand by generating leads and opportunities to get you out there following up, making deals and making money. If this sounds like you, then you're in the right place at the right time!

What if there was a way to have everything you need in one system so you can automatically generate leads and opportunities and broadcast your message to the connected planet while simultaneously having this same system doing all of your marketing, lead capture and follow-up? And what if there were people standing by to help you build your system?

This book will introduce you to a complete, proven, integrated system that combines tools and strategies to get you MORE LEADS AND OPPORTUNITIES, so you can close more deals and make more money.

By the time you finish reading this book and reviewing the videos available in a free series, you'll understand some new concepts and strategies for finding leads and opportunities and maybe even how to structure deals so you use no cash, no credit and no joint venture partners.

About The Author

Number one best-selling author, real estate investor and business consultant John A. McCabe has been a business consultant since 2004 and a real estate investor since 2009. John has leveraged his education and experience into that of a best-selling author, coach, mentor, speaker, systems and marketing expert. He is the author of Amazon number one best-seller "Rent to Own Revolution," the founder of ioffersolutions Real Estate Services Inc., Rent To Own Revolution Inc. and creator of the Rent To Own Revolution Biz Op, designed to automatically generate leads and opportunities to help investors control millions of dollars in real estate and generate a six-figure-per-year income.

John has had an impressive career as both a business consultant and real estate investor. Through his implementation of process, procedures, systems, technology and personnel he helped grow a company from $1.5 million to $7 million in just four years while dramatically increasing its bottom line. John then started ioffersolutions Real Estate Services and within two years had been involved in controlling over $10 million worth of real estate, generating him a six-figure-per-year income without ever using his own money or credit.

His unique and proven lead generating model combined with rent-to-own has provided his investors and homeowners above-average returns and all the benefits of investing in real estate with little to no risks to them. His vision is for his Biz Op System to help generate the leads and opportunities for a nation of real estate investors to control $100 billion worth of real estate.

Originally from Windsor, Nova Scotia, the Birthplace of Hockey, he studied business at Acadia University then moved to Edmonton, Alberta, where he currently lives and works. John gives credit to his parents, Gary and Shirley McCabe, and his real estate coach and mentor, Ross Lightle, for his desire to help and serve others. John enjoys fast-pitch softball and has won numerous provincial championships, and has competed at both the national championships and the ISC World Fastball Championship. He now spends his spare time golfing and travelling.

Follow The Author

You can follow John A. McCabe through his Social Media accounts.

Facebook.com/JohnAnthonyMcCabe

Facebook.com/ioffersolutions

Facebook.com/RentToOwnRevolution

Twitter.com/JohnAMcCabe

Youtube.com/user/JohnAnthonyMcCabe

Linkedin.com/in/JohnAnthonyMcCabe

Google.com/+JohnMcCabe

FREE Member's Area

To get FREE updates to this book, along with the accompanying videos, resources and materials referenced that will allow you to create your very own automated "SILVER BULLET" to help you control millions in real estate and generate a 6-figure yearly income

visit <u>www.InfiniteRealEstateRoi.com</u>

OR text your name and email to (587) 800-1551

OR Scan the QR Code

Acknowledgement

Everything that has happened to me up to this point in time, the successes, the struggles and the failures has molded and shaped me into the person I am today. I am thankful and grateful each and every day for my health, my family, my coaches, my partners and my friends. Life has not always been easy, there have been both ups and downs, but what has remained constant is the love and support of my parents, my coaches, partners and my true friends.

To Mom and Dad, I strive each and every day to make you proud of the person you have raised me to be.

To Ross, Neil and Barb, I am humbled and grateful you chose me to be part of something great.

To Heather and Hannah, you will always have my love and support in life.

To Jeff and Russell, I could never ask for better

friends. Your friendship and kindness both in good times and bad has meant more to me then you will ever realize.

To all my private coaching clients and certified consultants - I am humbled you have chosen me to help you achieve your goals.

Preface

Welcome, my name is John A. McCabe and I'm going to take you on a journey that teaches you how you can control over $10 million in real estate even if you have no cash, no credit, no joint venture partners, and even if you suffer from anxiety at just the thought of cold-calling a homeowner.

Now I realize that is a big and bold claim, and I want you to be skeptical. Having said that, I can promise that when you spend some time with this book and the companion videos, you'll see just how easy it can be to build a successful real estate investing business where you control and make money on other people's homes.

Since 2009 I've been building, tweaking and perfecting a system for my own personal real estate investing business that generates my business an abundance of leads and opportunities for homeowners wanting my company to take over their home. This allows me to make a great deal of money in the process. In this book, I'm about to give you the number one secret – something that really is the SILVER BULLET, SECRET FORMULA and MAGIC BUTTON all rolled into one – that can dramatically change your life and multiply the value of your real estate business.

Think about this: If you had an unlimited supply of leads and opportunities that all had the potential to be worth $40,000–$60,000 each, how would that change your life?

With the content in this book and the videos, you can be earning a six-figure income in your first year and be controlling millions of dollars of real estate. Even if you are lazy, slightly introverted, and flat broke with no cash, no credit or potential joint venture partners, you will have the knowledge you need to make things happen.

If you've been seeking and searching for years for the answer or the secret that can literally turn around your personal life and real estate investing business, you've found it.

Maybe you want to be able to quit your job soon but need to generate enough income to make that a reality. You want to create a business that is going to generate you wealth so you can live the life you've dreamed for yourself. One where you don't have to worry about money, where your family is taken care of, one of travel and quality time with your family.

Most people are drawn into the world of real estate investing by attending a seminar where they show you how easy it is to make money in this business. Maybe that is just how you entered into the industry; I know that's how I got involved.

The real estate investing seminar business is huge and gets a lot of people to spend money on courses and training with the promise that you can do this too. Well, unfortunately only 2–3 percent of the people who attend those courses go on to actually do anything in real estate investing. You see, my real estate coach and mentor, Ross Lightle, built and ran a company for 10 years that is now known as Rich Dad Education here in Canada. He has seen thousands of people come and go and invest a lot of money on their education, only to do nothing with it.

Why? Because it can be hard and people are inherently lazy. The investing part itself isn't hard; that is actually really easy. The hard part, and the biggest frustration almost every real estate investor has, is finding leads and opportunities that they can convert to deals. Real estate seminars teach you how to structure and analyze deals, not how to generate leads in today's environment.

I first built this system when I was faced with true hardship, uncertainty and was on the verge of financial ruin when I lost my consulting contract back in June 2009. It was a recession and I had put $40,000 on my credit cards to take some real estate investing courses just three months earlier.

By mid-June I had taken three courses and had just started paying off the credit cards I used to pay for the courses. On June 29, 2009, the owners of the company came into my office and informed me that the next day would be my last. We were still in a recession and they had let go almost all staff except for essential personnel.

Talk about a shock! I looked at my bank account and had enough money to last me for three months. Because it was a recession, it was going to be very hard to find another contract or even a job. I decided since I invested in the real estate investing courses I'd better go down that road. However, I had no money. Since I was self-employed, I couldn't qualify for any mortgages and I didn't have any joint venture partners. Oh, and I'm somewhat of an introvert so cold-calling homeowners gave me anxiety and was out of the question.

Fortunately, I had gained some marketing knowledge from a previous venture I was involved in between 2000–2004 so I had an idea what to do online to get my phone ringing. I then went ahead and put together a strategy for attracting homeowners to contact me regarding their property. Within the first week I had several meetings and continued to have meetings each and every week.

Within the first month I took over my first property and on September 1, 2009, I made $5,000 and was set to make $600 cash flow for the next three years. From that point on I took over at least one property a month for the next 24 months that made me between $5,000–$7,500 instantly and between $100–$500 per month in cash flow for the next 3–4 years each.

In two years I was controlling more than 24 properties worth over $10 million dollars and was making a six-figure income each year. Not bad for a lazy introvert with zero cash, zero credit and no joint venture partners. I will admit, after my first year in the business I was attracting people with money who wanted to invest with me, and I did let them. I could have continued on without them but partnering with them just meant I could make more money.

Throughout this book I'm going to explain the "silver bullet" I've spent five years perfecting. This silver bullet gets homeowners contacting me on a daily basis to inquire about my company taking over their property. There is never a need to find deals and opportunities; they just come flooding in every single day.

Let me be crystal clear, this is not just some website, Facebook page, Kijiji ad, SEO gimmick, etc. This is a complete overall strategy that starts with understanding your ideal target market and leading them down the path to contact you for an appointment, then getting them to say YES.

This book will focus on the two components I have used to build a successful real estate investing company controlling over $10 million in real estate and making a consistent six-figure income.

First and foremost, you don't need cash, credit or even JV partners to control millions of dollars in real estate when you understand the power of the option contract and how to use it.

Second, having a system that generates you an abundance of leads of homeowners willing to give you control over their property allows you to then convert those leads into an opportunity to make money and build a successful real estate investing business.

Since 2009 I've invested over $100,000 in education and other people's systems to perfect this model, and spent one full year beta-testing a component of the system with some brand-new real estate investors just so I can share this hard-earned knowledge and wisdom with you. In that one year those investors were able to control 13 properties worth over $4 million, and they're scheduled to make around half a million dollars over the course of three years.

If for some reason I lost everything tomorrow I'd be right here with you using this information to build myself another system that would generate an abundance of leads and opportunities. With those I could rebuild my real estate investing business to its current level in less than a year.

Enjoy this book and the videos and I will see you on the other side of the screen.

John McCabe

Excellent!

Good. You've taken the first step. You have this book and you're reading it.

Even if you've read other real estate investing books, this one is different because until just a few weeks ago, much of what is discussed in this book wasn't possible.

If you use what's here, it will forever change the way you think about real estate investing, generating leads and opportunities and building a business.

I know you're super busy, overwhelmed and looking for ways to get ahead.

My guess is you want a lifestyle change, more control over what you do and how you do it... You want to do more deals, make more money, spend more time with family and friends and travel more... and maybe you're just getting started....

The first thing you should do is sign up for the free videos – details are below. When you register for the free videos, you'll also get notified when this book is updated. It's a work in progress and will change based on the feedback and comments I receive.

John A. McCabe

Next, attend one of our "livecasts" – high-quality, interactive online events. When you register for the free videos, you'll be registered automatically and receive an invitation link to join me. There, you'll meet me and have a chance to learn more about everything we talk about in this book firsthand with live-chat and interactivity. These livecasts are fun and you'll learn a ton.

Next, skim through this book and read whatever jumps out and speaks to you. I'm a big believer in trusting intuition. Trust your gut.

I'll share some transformational stories that will help you learn more, faster. I hope you'll be inspired by them and use the lessons to get more results and impact in your life.

Everything in this book works – in fact, it is constantly evolving and being refined. I built my real estate investing business around these strategies and systems from start to finish in less than a month. This same model has been used successfully by thousands of other customers all over the world. It can work for you too.

Here's a warning: Don't delay. Take imperfect action. The Internet and the web are growing at an amazing pace. The world will continue to get more competitive; people will feel even more overwhelmed and get busier. Right now, it's easier and more affordable than ever before to be seen, heard and found.

But that might change a day, a week, a month or a year from now and the sooner you get started and implement the strategies found in "Infinite Real Estate ROI," you can accomplish your dreams by getting more leads, making more deals, controlling more real estate and making more money.

Contents

Section 1: The Strategy

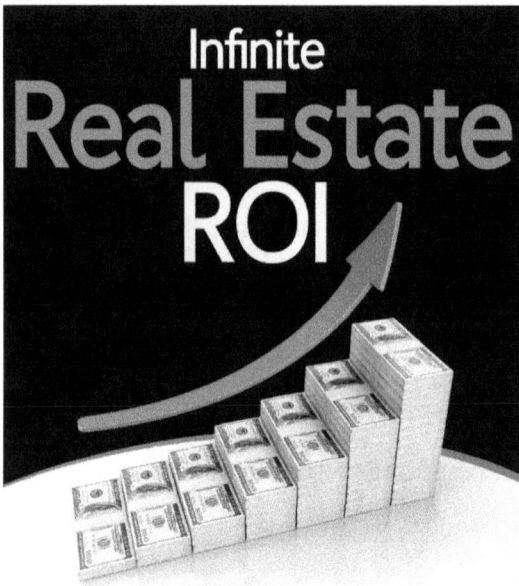

Chapter 1

WHAT YOU CAN EXPECT IN THIS BOOK

There is a good chance that if you are reading this book you were drawn to the real estate investing world to make a great deal of money, generate and protect your wealth, create a better life for you and your family and for financial freedom. Freedom to do what you want, when you want and with whom you want. Freedom, which is what we all seek to some degree.

This book will build your real estate business – fast. Whether you already have a successful real estate investing business or you are just getting started, this is a recipe for generating leads and opportunities that you can turn into real money with no cash, no credit and no joint venture partners. Think about it – what if people came to you specifically for you to take over their property? What if you could create such a powerful system that made you more money than you do right now, without ever having to worry about cash, credit or partners?

There is a process, a formula, a method, if you

will, that can get you there. I've created and honed that formula since 2009, and I'm going to share it with you in this book.

There is no theory in this book. Everything I'm going to teach you is based on real-world results. This method was created through trial and error, a huge investment into learning which strategies work and which ones don't, and real-life experience.

The results have been staggering. I started my business while deep in despair and facing sure financial uncertainty and I've gone on to control over $10 million dollars of real estate and consistently generate a six-figure-a-year income. And more to the point, I've helped a couple of brand-new investors use the exact same system to control over $4 million worth of real estate and generate a six-figure income from zero in one short year.

The funny thing is, as I reflect back, it all happened accidentally. I didn't set out to build a formula or method or become a leader in the industry. In fact, when I started out, I had enough money to last three months. I had to make something happen fast while at the same time overcome my obstacle of being an introvert and having anxiety at the thought of calling a homeowner or knocking on their door.

The "silver bullet" method is really about bringing two components together to make one powerful system with the focus of number two being the strategy in number one.

1. The power of the option contract: The option contract is probably the most powerful contract one can have in real estate. As the name suggests, it gives you options. Maybe you will buy the home, maybe you won't. But until that time comes, you control the fate of the house, and when you combine the option contract with a lease, you have the ability to make money with someone else's property without the need of buying the home.

2. Complete Marketing System: This is more than just having a website or Facebook page. This is about your positioning, your story and having a complete strategy that works in conjunction with the option contract. It would take into account the following:

    a. Understanding the pains, fears, frustrations or ambitions of the homeowner who wants to sell or rent out their home.

    b. Creating your hook and your story – Your why as well as your what; your

personal narrative so others will know, like and trust you
c. Writing effective copy for your marketing materials
d. Generating traffic – flyers, ads, social media, optimizing for search engines
e. Building your online presence and marketing material: website/squeeze page, social media,
f. Presenting to the homeowner effectively
g. Closing the deal - contracts

In the first section of this book I will get into the lease option strategy, possible exit strategies and how much money you can make using this strategy. In the second section I will explain how to build your system that automates almost every aspect of your business to keep the leads and opportunities constantly flowing in for you to follow up.

To get FREE updates to this book, along with the accompanying videos, resources and materials referenced that will allow you to create your very own automated "SILVER BULLET" to help you control millions in real estate and generate a 6-figure yearly income

visit www.InfiniteRealEstateRoi.com

OR text your name and email to (587) 800-1551

OR Scan the QR Code

Chapter 2

THE POWER OF THE OPTION

My journey into real estate investing started back in 2009 because of my constant love of travel. As a self-employed contractor, every time I wanted to travel and take a vacation I would come home to zero income. Being self-employed didn't give me the luxury of having vacation days. Oh, I could take vacation days whenever I wanted, but I wasn't getting paid to be away.

For that reason alone I started investigating solutions that would pay me while I didn't work and real estate investing is what caught my attention. I then started reading books about investing and bought several books by Robert Kiyosaki in his Rich Dad series. It was during a two-week vacation in Europe in January 2009 that my friend Heather sent me a message letting me know there was going to be a FREE two-hour Rich Dad Poor Dad seminar coming to Edmonton just after I returned from holidays. I asked Heather to sign me up so I could attend.

If you have ever gone to any of those free events

I'm sure you know how this story goes. During the free event, I signed up for a $500 weekend event, which led me to signing up for $40,000 worth of courses, coaching and mentorship. It didn't take long for me to max out every single credit card I had in order to get involved. For me, I was drawn into the dream of making big money quick, and doing it with no money like they showed in the examples.

The first thing I want to stress is that even though enrolling in $40,000 worth of training worked out for me, it is not something I would ever advocate to anyone wanting to do this business. For the most part, people just get overwhelmed with all the information and then don't act on anything they've learned.

I suggest educating yourself through books like this one and my Amazon number one best-seller "Rent To Own Revolution," www.RentToOwnRevolution.com/Book, as well as videos, which are no to low cost. You also may want to start attending real estate investment networking groups and take some individual courses. Then, I suggest working with a coach or mentor to help you decide what aspect of real estate investing you want to get into.

Between March and June of 2009 I had taken three

courses with the education company and was analyzing properties and opportunities in my spare time. I had also picked my company name, built my website and optimized it for the services I was offering. Back then optimizing a website was so much easier than it is today. As of the time of writing this book, content with a heavy emphasis on engagement is the new SEO in the Internet world.

Like most things, it takes time to get your website optimized and to hold one or more positions on the first page of Google for the search terms people use to find a solution to their pain, fear, frustration or ambition.

The third course I took in June 2009 was called Lease Option. It was in this course I was really shown how this no-money-down real estate strategy could be duplicated over and over in almost any situation. It was during that course that I recognized the power of the lease-option contract and how someone like me could use it to generate a great deal of money in real estate. That was exactly what I was looking for – something that would complement the money I was making from my business consulting.

You know the old saying, don't put all your eggs in one basket? Well, I didn't heed that advice and only had one consulting client that I had worked for over the past four-and-a-half years. If you recall, in 2009 we were in a recession and the writing was on the wall. The company had laid off almost all its workforce and there was very little work going on, so on June 29, 2009, the owners of the company gave me my one-day notice.

Wow, talk about some scary times. I had been self-employed and hadn't held a job for over eight years. Because it was a recession, the chance of getting a job or a new contract was going to be very slim. I had enough money saved to last three months, credit card debt of $40,000 and all the typical monthly payments a person has like vehicle, rent, insurance, etc.

On July 1, 2009, I made the decision I was going to immerse myself in real estate investing and do it full-time, with the emphasis on lease-optioning properties then helping people who don't qualify for a traditional mortgage get into home ownership through my rent-to-own program.

In real estate the option contract is probably the most powerful contract available to you as an investor. The main reason is that it gives you options, just as the name suggests. It gives you the ability to control property without ever taking ownership of the property. When you add in the lease, you have full control over the owner's property.

The owner remains on title but you have the option to purchase it in the future. Now, with that option you have the ability to prevent the homeowner from selling the property from underneath you, and you have the ability to prevent the owner from refinancing the property and putting it further in debt. Controlling the property really means that you have the ability to make money on the property.

At the end, you have the option as to what you want to do. You can buy the home or you can walk away – it is completely up to you. If you have a tenant buyer in the home in the case of a rent-to-own or there is a lot of equity in the property, you would want to buy the property. Depending on your contracts, you may need to do a simultaneous close, which is getting harder to do. This is where you buy the home from the owner at the exact same time you sell it to the tenant buyer. You never actually need to qualify for the mortgage or need any cash. The contracts I currently use allows me enables me to close directly between the owner and the tenant buyer. I don't have to worry about getting my money, the contracts protect my interest.

For more details on lease-option contracts get a copy of my book "Rent To Own Revolution," www.RentToOwnRevolution.com/Book, where I go into greater detail about contracts. Understanding and having the ability to lease-option a property is one of the most powerful strategies and tools you can have in your investor tool belt. In the next chapter I'm going show you what situations you can use the option contracts in, then I will get into how much money can be made with this strategy.

Many old-school real estate investors or investors who only focus on buy-rent-hold and refuse to embrace the lease-option strategy are missing out on so much potential money in real estate. True wealth in real estate comes from owning property for over 10 years and benefitting from the mortgage pay-down and pulling out the equity tax-free. For many who get into this industry, that is their long-term goal. However, not everyone has the cash to get started, or they run out of money after buying one or two properties.

For most people getting into this business, they don't want to wait 10-plus years to quit their job or be financially free. They want to make things happen fast! This is an instant gratification society, after all. What I typically tell real estate investors who only want to focus on buy-rent-hold strategies is, why not learn another strategy and build a system that can make you a substantial amount of money in a short period of time so you can buy more buy-rent-hold properties and get access to deals and opportunities that you don't find through a Realtor or MLS?

This "silver bullet" method and strategy has generated me some amazing leads, deals and opportunities that I either capitalized on myself or got the homes under contract and wholesaled the contracts to some other investors who were looking for good deals and had the available cash and credit to make the deal happen.

I have made over $100,000 since 2009 just wholesaling the opportunities that came to me directly as a result of the homeowners contacting me through my marketing system. This was on the opportunities I didn't have the cash for at the time or just didn't have the time to tackle. They were great opportunities and I knew someone would want them, so I put them under contract and sold the contracts.

Since the homeowners are contracting you directly, you are able to cut out all the middlemen such as Realtors and other investors. Homeowners who come through the marketing system also know exactly what it is you want to do, which is rent their home for 2–3 years then buy the home.

Using the lease-option contracts combined with a system that generates a constant flow of leads and opportunities has enabled me to build a successful real estate investment business controlling over $10 million worth of real estate and make a six-figure-per-year income with no cash, no credit and no partners in only 2 short years.

It was an earlier version of this same system I leased out to two of my private coaching clients, Trevor and Nina, who were both new investors just getting started in real estate. They both wanted to build a business quickly. To verify the system would work for anyone, regardless of how much experience they had, I used them as a beta test for one year. During that year, with no assistance from me at all, they received more leads and opportunities then they could handle and managed to put together 13 deals controlling over $4 million in real estate with a profit potential of $500,000 over a four-year period. That works out to an average of $125,000 per year.

Not bad for a couple of new investors. The majority of their time was spent following up on leads and opportunities and closing on deals instead of spending that time just hunting down opportunities like almost every other investor was doing.

The quickest and least expensive method for you to learn how to do rent-to-own is to pick up a copy of my book "Rent To Own Revolution" by going to www.RentToOwnRevolution.com/book. In that book I go into great detail how the rent-to-own business works, how you structure the deals, and how to calculate the numbers for both the homeowner as well as the tenant buyer. You also have access to specific services like a contract service where we create the contracts for you and application services for your potential tenant buyers.

To get FREE updates to this book, along with the accompanying videos, resources and materials referenced that will allow you to create your very own automated "SILVER BULLET" to help you control millions in real estate and generate a 6-figure yearly income

visit www.InfiniteRealEstateRoi.com

OR text your name and email to
(587) 800-1551

OR Scan the QR Code

Chapter 3

EXIT STRATEGIES

Just as you do when you are analyzing deals and opportunities, you need to look at the various exit strategies, their ROI and which one you are going to choose prior to making an offer on the property. It is no different when you are using the lease-option strategy instead of the traditional purchase strategy. You must be aware of the exit strategies available to you and determine which one best suits your situation at the time.

Of course we are all aware of the strategy to lease-option the property then turn around and put someone in the home on the rent-to-own scenario, where you have your built-in tenant and buyer all in one. This is by far the best strategy in most cases.

Lease Option – Fix – Sell

Sometimes you come across situations where the homeowner only has six or nine months left on the term of the mortgage and they aren't going to qualify for renewal. In most of these cases the homeowner will try to sell the home; however, if the home is one that needs fixing, then the chances of it selling are going to be slim.

Depending upon the amount of equity in the home, how much work needs to be done and how much you can force the appreciation, it may be a home that you would generally associate with a buy-fix-sell situation. But my philosophy is, why buy it if you can control it and not need any credit or qualifying? On many occasions I have taken over homes like this through the lease option, so instead of buying the home I take over the payments for the next six to nine months. The home needs to be vacant for me to enter into this type of arrangement, obviously, because we are going to go in and reno the home.

Keep in mind there is a lot of analysis that needs to go into determining if this scenario works. You need to be clear on your analysis, you need to be 100 percent sure on your financials and estimates, and you need to err on the side of conservative with respect to the after-repair value. You need to know that if you take on this project you are going to be able to complete the reno on time and on budget and be able to sell the home for your asking price in the time allotted. Remember, you may only have six to nine months to complete the project from start to closing the sale.

I always approach these strategies with a couple different end scenarios in mind. We know that we must sell or purchase the home by the end of the term, being six to nine months. During the renovation I am looking to find an investor who might want to buy the home from us at a discount, meaning we sell to recover our costs and make a little money in the project, and they in turn allow us to lease-option the home from them so we can turn it into a three-year rent-to-own.

Another thing I'm doing at the same time is structuring the lease-option paperwork so that if needed I can allocate all my reno costs as my option consideration money to be used as my down payment and purchase the home myself. This is a great way to buy the properties that you are going to buy, fix and hold on to as long-term rentals. Instead of shelling out the 20-plus percent down payment to buy the home then paying the costs of the renovations, increasing the cash you have in the project, you lease-option the home, pay for the renovations and use those renovation costs as your down payment.

One thing to remember: you need to be able to justify the value of the work so you will need to get two or three written quotes for the value of the work. This is where it comes in handy if you do the work yourself and get some contractors who do the same type of work but are on the high end of the scale for pricing.

If you raise the value of the home enough you even may be able to structure getting some cash back out of the deal when you purchase the home yourself.

Lease Option – Fix – Rent-to-Own

This scenario is very much like the one above, but you may have a much longer timeframe to the term of the homeowner's mortgage, so it gives you the ability to rent-to-own the property. Normally I like to have at least a three-year term on my lease options, which means a two-year with a 12-month extension if needed, or a three-year with a 12-month extension if needed. The reason is that most people need three years or less to fix their credit situation, unless they are still in a bankruptcy situation or still in consumer proposal. But if they have been discharged from either of those or just have bad credit, we can get them a traditional mortgage in less than three years, provided they are working with our credit coach and mortgage broker.

An example is this bungalow located only blocks from West Edmonton Mall in Edmonton. The owner inherited a problem from his dad when his dad died. The home had not been updated in over 30 years, was financed to the value of the home in its current condition and the owner was actually behind in payments as a result of having to carry the property.

The owner, Walter, just wanted someone to take the property off his hands. Fortunately enough he had just over three years left owing on the mortgage. I made an agreement with Walter to lease-option his property for the cost of the monthly payments and to buy the home at the end of the three-year term for what was left owing on the mortgage.

The home would require about $20,000–$25,000 in renovations in order to get it up to show-ready condition. We are talking about new kitchen, bathrooms, flooring, paint, fixtures etc. At that point of time it was not a project I could take on. Fortunately, however, I did have the exit strategy already, which was a tenant buyer named Stacy who was looking for a rent-to-own in the area, had $10,000 down payment and needed 2–3 years to qualify for a traditional mortgage.

It was just at that time an investor was referred to me who had some cash but couldn't qualify for a mortgage. Her name was Doreen and she only understood buy-rent-hold as a strategy, definitely not lease-option. After I explained to her that she would control this home for the next three years and needed to invest about $20,000 to renovate the property, $7,500 for my fee and about $3,000 in arrears, she could turn around and recover $10,000 of her investment back as soon as Stacy moved in, make $700 per month cash flow and net out another $25,000 when the house sold at the end of the three years. In total she was going to make over $80,000 gross profit and $50,000 net after recovering her $30,000 investment.

For the homeowner, they were happy – they had their problem taken care of. For Stacy, she was happy – she got a new place to live and the chance to become a homeowner. Doreen was happy because she discovered a new way to do real estate investing that could make her a great deal of money since she couldn't qualify for any more houses, and of course I was happy because I made $7,500 for putting all the pieces together. As of the month I am writing this book, the deal is scheduled to close, and after speaking to the mortgage broker, I can confirm it is on track to do so.

Save Someone from Foreclosure with Lease Option, Then Rent the House Out

As in the previous example, the lease option can be used to save someone from foreclosure. It is one of the best situations I have found to use a lease option, especially when there are several years left on the term of the mortgage, some equity in the home and the homeowner just wants to leave.

One such example is the house that I'm currently living in. In 2011 the homeowner contacted me and was going into foreclosure. I met with the owner, Ron, and viewed the home, which is located in a new area on the west side of Edmonton called Glastonbury. The home was huge, 2,300 sq ft on the top two levels, and the basement was completely finished. The home had four beds, three-and-a-half baths and a mortgage balance of $454,000. The home at that time would have been valued slightly higher but the homeowner had pets and the carpets were damaged and the walls had the original paint from when the house was built in 2007.

This home was quite far along in the stages of foreclosure; however, the owner still had control of the home and it hadn't been put up for a forced sale as of yet. After meeting with the owner and getting all the details, I proceeded forward with taking over control of the property. That meant paying out arrears of $17,000 and taking over the mortgage and tax payments, which were just over

$2,200 per month. This was an expensive proposition but I knew there was going to be lots of upside to the home.

I put the home up for rent-to-own immediately after taking control of the property and moved in while I was trying to get someone to take it over. After carrying the home for about four months I decided to find a great family to put in the home that were looking for a rental. The costs to carry the home were more than I wanted to pay, even living there myself.

I found a great family that was willing to rent the home for the duration of the term I had with the owner, less a couple of months for us to get it show-ready to sell. Well the renters stayed in the home and did a great job of caring for the place, but even with that, after seven years of people living in the home, it was time for new paint and new carpet. On May 1, 2014, I took back the home after the tenants moved out and proceeded to invest $20,000 for painting, carpet and carrying costs for two months. Now I was into the home for about $40,000 and the mortgage balance was down to $425,000 for the payout. That meant I was into the property for $465,000. After some market research there were properties selling in the area for around $475,000-$485,000, which I thought just wasn't a good enough return on my investment.

I then decided to contact the owner to discuss the situation, since the mortgage was due for renewal. I had kept in touch with the owner on and off during the past three years and he was very happy that I'd helped him with his problem, so we had a good relationship. I explained the situation to him, which was that I was into the home for about $40,000 and I would be lucky to get my money back if I sold the house today. I wasn't in the business of helping people and losing money so I asked him if he would accompany me to the bank and sign a mortgage renewal on the home, giving me more time for both the mortgage to get paid down and the value of the home to rise.

He agreed and we signed a four-year renewal at an interest rate of 2.89 percent, which dropped the mortgage by $300 per month. It was right around that time that I was looking for a place to live; you see, I typically live in the properties I take over where I can live cheaper then rent and have the benefits of mortgage pay-down, just as if I actually owned the house. I decided to move in and still reside here…. Until I decide I want to make money on this house or feel like moving again.

If I were to rent-to-own this house for the last three years of the term I would be able to get at least

$15,000 up front for a non-refundable option consideration payment, I would be able to make $500 per month in cash flow, and net – after I recovered my $40,000 investment – $55,000 when the house sold. So all in, I would make about $90,000 just on this one house in that three-year time frame. Hmm, makes me think I need to find another place to live and rent-to-own this house.

But even if I didn't rent-to-own and stayed here or rented it out for the next three or four years, then sold it at the end of the term, there is nothing stopping me from asking the owner to renew the mortgage again; it costs him nothing. It would only be an issue if it were preventing him from qualifying for anything else in the future. At the end of the term of the mortgage, the buyout for the home will be roughly $395,000 on a home that would be worth around $500,000 or more by then. Provided there isn't any major repairs or maintenance required, I would easily recapture my investment and make a nice profit on the sale of the home.

You can see through some of the examples in this chapter there are variety of exit strategies available to you when you have control of the home. You don't just have to rent-to-own, but it is generally the most lucrative. I also showed you how you can make money just putting the deal together and selling it to another investor for a fee because you were able to lease-option the property. You can also help a lot of people facing foreclosure and even find yourself a place to call home. You get to benefit from the mortgage pay-down and recapture the equity when you sell the home, just as if you owned the place.

The lease-option strategy can be very powerful and is very versatile. Once you have control of the property you have multiple exit strategies and multiple ways to make money.

To get FREE updates to this book, along with the accompanying videos, resources and materials referenced that will allow you to create your very own automated "SILVER BULLET" to help you control millions in real estate and generate a 6-figure yearly income

visit www.InfiniteRealEstateRoi.com

OR text your name and email to
(587) 800-1551

OR Scan the QR Code

Chapter 4

SHOW ME THE MONEY

As you have seen from the examples in the last chapter, the opportunities are endless when you control the home. Yes, in many of those examples it took cash to either get the homeowner out of foreclosure or cash needed to fix up the home in order to either sell or rent-to-own the home. Those were just some of the situations and exit strategies you can use with lease-option. But by far, the most common use of the lease option is when you take over someone's home that is already in good shape and turn it into a rent-to-own. In this chapter we will talk specifically about those scenarios and I will show you the money!

The areas in your town or city you target will dictate the types of homes where you have the opportunity to lease-option. I recommend targeting newer areas, places built within the last 5–10 years for two reasons.

First, generally the homes are newer and because of that will be in higher demand by your tenant buyer. The second reason is that these homeowners have less mortgage pay-down, so recovering their initial investment through a traditional sale is more difficult, especially if they bought the home at the peak of the market in 2006–2007 or they only put 5 percent down when they bought the home.

Anyone who only put 5 percent down would have mortgage insurance fees (CMHC fees in Canada) tacked on to the mortgage, which means the home is financed in reality at 97–98 percent of its cost. Even though the market has recovered from the downturn, after the peak of 2007 the home typically hasn't gone up, nor the mortgage gone down, enough for a homeowner to walk away with all their investment back when they sell traditionally through a realtor.

I will get more into the homeowner's motivation for getting involved in this type of scenario in the next chapter when we discuss the pains, fears, frustrations and ambitions of the homeowners. In this chapter, remember I am going to show you the money on a traditional lease-option with the homeowner and then turning it into a rent-to-own with a tenant buyer. This is generally called a sandwich lease-option.

As mentioned, this strategy will generally account for over 90 percent of the lease-options you do. The main reasons include not requiring much cash, any partners, any renovation skills, or the need to qualify for a mortgage.

When a homeowner agrees to rent you their property for two to three years and give you the option to purchase the home at the end, you are going to need to put together the contracts. As mentioned, I go into great detail in my book "Rent To Own Revolution" about contracts; however, in order to make the option contract valid you will need to give the homeowner an amount of money. I typically give the homeowner a cheque for $100 just to make the contracts legal. You can use $1 or you can use $1,000 or more – it is completely up to you. But there must be an exchange in order for the contract to be legal.

I realize I said you don't need any cash for this strategy, but in the big scheme of things $100 isn't much. And like I said, you can use $1 if you want. So just go cash in your beer bottles, wine bottles or pop bottles from the garage if you need to raise the $1.

OK, now it is important that we use an actual property so I can give you some actual numbers to get an idea of how much you can expect to make in these deals. I'm going to give you two different examples. The first one was a one-year rent-to-own, which is quite rare and on the low scale for the amount of money you can make, and the second one was a three-year deal, which is closer to the high end of a typical deal.

The first home is a three bedroom, two-and-a-half bathroom 2009 townhouse I lease-optioned from the homeowner, Erich. Now Erich wanted more time for his mortgage to pay down; as well, he didn't want to pay the hefty $12,500 Realtor commissions if he sold the home he had only owned for two years. Erich signed a three-year lease-option agreement with me; however, in those agreements I can purchase the home anytime within the three years. Erich wanted to benefit from the mortgage pay-down and save himself the commissions so he agreed to lease the property to me for $1,490 per month (the actual cost of carrying the property) and I had the option to buy the home for $277,000 (slightly below the current estimated value of the property at that time). In a later chapter I will go through negotiating with the homeowner and coming up with the figures to offer them.

After showing the home to several interested parties, a young family – the parents' names were Mike and Jodi – decided to take the home. After putting Mike and Jodi through the application process, my mortgage broker and credit coach told me they qualified for the price point and they only needed one year, just time to build up their down payment.

Based on all that information, I put together the contracts for Mike and Jodi. Those contracts had them paying an initial option consideration of $7,500, monthly rent of $1500 and monthly option consideration of $650 that got added to their initial option consideration to total $15,300, to be used as their down payment on a purchase price of $305,000.

So how much money did I make on this one-year deal?

Initial option: $7,500 - $100 (paid to Erich to make contract valid) = $7400
Monthly: ($1500 + $650 - $1490) x 12 = $7,920
Sale: $305,000 - $15,300 - $277,000 = $12,700

Total: $7,400 + $7,920 + $12,700 = $28,020

Not bad for the 5–10 hours' worth of work it actually took me from start to finish on this deal. If I had known going into the deal with Erich it was going to be only one year I would have negotiated a lower purchase price.

This is a very low deal when it comes to doing rent-to-own.

The next deal is more in line with what you can expect from a three-year rent-to-own.

The house is a 2007-built 2100 sq ft three bedroom, two-and-a-half bathroom home in Leduc. The owners are Dipak, his wife and his son TJ. It was TJ's home but he moved out and they wanted to rent out the home for the duration of the term left on the mortgage so they didn't incur any payout penalties. I rented the home from them for $1,800 per month and have a purchase at the end of the term for $430,000.

A great couple, Jonathon and Randine, were interested in getting into home ownership. Their situation is quite common here in Edmonton, that being Randine had amazing credit but couldn't qualify for the price of the home on her own, while Jonathon made twice as much money but had some blemishes on his credit that would take a couple of years to fix. So after they went through the application process with our mortgage broker and credit coach, they were approved to buy the home for $479,000 at the end of their three-year term.

Rent for houses similar to that was around the $2,200-per-month range and based on them putting $10,000 down as their initial option consideration payment they would need to make monthly option payments of $400 in order to have their minimum

5 percent down payment by the end of the rent-to-own term.

So how much money did we make on this three-year deal?

Initial option: $10,000 - $100 = $9,900
Monthly: ($2200 + $400 - $1800) x 36 = $28,800
Sale at End: $479,000 - $24,400 - $430,000 = $24,600

Total: $9,900 + $28,800 + $24,600 = $63,300

So over the three-year period this one property will make me $63,300. That is quite typical of a three-year deal, to be making around the $50,000–$60,000 range. Sometimes there isn't as much made on the monthly cash flow – we can see this one was $800 per month – but there is more made at the end of the deal. Regardless, it usually works out to around $60,000 for a three-year deal based on the method I have created to capture the lead and opportunity and present it to the homeowner, which I will talk about in a later chapter.

You can see, just in these two examples I was controlling over $700,000 worth of real estate and was scheduled to make just over $90,000 total. I don't know of any other strategy that allows you control that much real estate with no cash (yes, it did take $100 per property, but that was returned quickly), no credit (I didn't need to qualify), and I didn't need to find any joint venture partners to get involved in doing these deals.

How to Make $10,000 Per Month Only Doing Two Deals Per Year

I can tell you right now, I'm not even trying to do any lease options or generate any leads and opportunities but my system keeps on working. It works so well it forces me to meet with homeowners each and every month. Not as many as if I actually made an effort, mind you, but for someone who is doing absolutely nothing to generate leads I've still put together six lease options this year and it is only September 1.

But what if you tried even less than me? I'm not sure how that is possible, but what if instead of doing six deals per year you only did two deals? I'm thinking I could find a zombie from The Walking Dead and I could get him to close on two lease options with owners, provided he didn't eat them first. But seriously, when you have leads and opportunities coming to you every week that want to meet with you so you can present them with your solution, you are going to land at least two homeowners in the course of the year.

So if you only did two deals a year, what would that look like and mean for your family? Well, here is the scenario based on the three-year example we went through previously.

Year #1

Deal # 1 (completed in March)

Option Consideration $10,000

Rent Differential ($800 / M x 9M) $7,200

Deal # 2 (completed in August)

Option Consideration   10,000

Rent Differential ($800 / M x 4M) $3,200

Total Income in Year #1 $30,400 or $2,533/M

Year #2

Deal #1 Rent Differential ($800 / M x 12M) $9,600

Deal #2 Rent Differential ($800 / M x 12M) $9,600

Deal # 3 (completed in March)

Option Consideration $10,000

Rent Differential ($800 / M x 9M) $7,200

Deal # 4 (completed in August)

Option Consideration	$10,000
Rent Differential ($800 / M x 4M)	$3,200
Total Income in Year #2	$49,600 or $4,133/M

Year #3

Deal #1 Rent Differential ($800 / M x 12M)	$9,600
Deal #2 Rent Differential ($800 / M x 12M)	$9,600
Deal #3 Rent Differential ($800 / M x 12M)	$9,600
Deal #4 Rent Differential ($800 / M x 12M)	$9,600
Deal # 5 (completed in March)	
Option Consideration	$10,000
Rent Differential ($800 / M x 9M)	$7,200
Deal # 6 (completed in August)	
Option Consideration	$10,000
Rent Differential ($800 / M x 4M)	$3,200
Total Income in Year #3	$68,800 or $5,733/M

Year #4

Deal #1 Profit at Closing	$24,600
Deal #2 Profit at Closing	$24,600
Deal #3 Rent Differential ($800 / M x 12M)	$9,600
Deal #4 Rent Differential ($800 / M x 12M)	$9,600
Deal #5 Rent Differential ($800 / M x 12M)	$9,600
Deal #6 Rent Differential ($800 / M x 12M)	$9,600
Deal #7 (completed in March)	
Option Consideration	$10,000
Rent Differential ($800 / M x 9M)	$7,200
Deal # 8 (completed in August)	
Option Consideration	$10,000
Rent Differential ($800 / M x 4M)	$3,200
Total Income in Year #4	$118,000 or $9,833/M

OK, as you can see you didn't quite make $10,000 per month, but you were darn close. Not a bad part-time gig for only doing two deals per year on a consistent, persistent basis.

Now I can hear all the skeptics right now saying, "But John, the homes in our area aren't worth that much." And you may be right for your area. So here are some numbers you can use on a typical home worth $300,000 today. I would collect $7,500 minimum for the option consideration. Based on that I would make $450 per month cash flow and at the end of the deal I would make $30,000. Based on those numbers the total income for Year 4 would be $101,850 or $8,488 per month. If that's the case and $10,000 is the goal, you may have to be slightly more energetic than a zombie and close on three deals per year, which would get you over the $150,000-per-year mark, or $12,500 per month.

When I first started I did one deal per month for the first 24 months, controlling over $10 million worth of real estate and easily making a six-figure income per year. Today, I don't do nearly as much and am very selective with respect to the properties I pick and the deals I do. The majority of my time is spent working with my private coaching clients, building systems for them and helping them create their own real estate investment business with no cash, no credit and no partners.

So how much is a lead or opportunity worth to you? Well as you have seen from the examples, the one-year deal was worth about $30,000 while the three-year deals are worth between $50,000–$60,000. So the question becomes, if each lead and opportunity has the potential to be worth $60,000, then how much are you willing to pay to get those leads coming in each and every week? To give you an idea what they are worth, I typically charge a fee between $7,500–$10,000 to investors for the leads that I have lease-optioned so the investors can go off and make $50,000–$60,000.

Remember Trevor and Nina, the two new investors who wanted to get into real estate investing and build a business with no money, no credit and no JV partners? They were the ones who leased out an early version of the silver bullet model I'm talking about in this book. You know, the ones that went on to control over $4 million worth of real estate with a profit potential of over $500,000 in just one year from the leads my system generated? Well, for the privilege of using my system they paid me $25,000 for one year. Was it worth it? Based on receiving the profit over a four-year period, it works out to be a 500 percent ROI, which is the annual return on their investment. I'm not sure if your buy-rent-hold properties are generating that much, or where else you could get $4 million worth of properties for only $25,000. It doesn't matter which way you look at it – it was a great deal for them and well worth the money they paid.

Here's the best part for you: The system they used, which I have improved upon and perfected, is the same one I'm going to lay out and explain through the rest of this book. I needed to lay the groundwork behind the power of the lease option, how you can use it, what the exit strategies are and potentially how much money you can make. Now, it's all about the system that will generate a steady flow of leads and opportunities that you can meet with to present them your solution.

A small amount of work on your part will drive traffic to your lead generating or squeeze page, where you will entice the homeowner to give you their name and email in exchange for something they deem to have value to them. Typically this is a video, video series, e-book, or report. This is called an "ethical bribe." There is an exchange going on: their contact information for your content.

Once the exchange has taken place, the system will capture the lead, educate the homeowner, follow up automatically, and get them to take action and book an appointment for you to come and walk through your presentation. Once you have your system built, it will automate almost every aspect of the process.

To get FREE updates to this book, along with the accompanying videos, resources and materials referenced that will allow you to create your very own automated "SILVER BULLET" to help you control millions in real estate and generate a 6-figure yearly income

visit www.InfiniteRealEstateRoi.com

OR text your name and email to (587) 800-1551

OR Scan the QR Code

Section 2: The Message

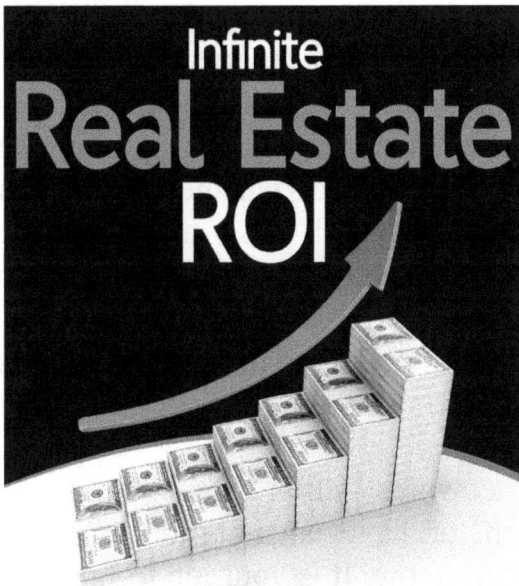

Chapter 5

WHY WOULD A HOME OWNER DO THIS?

Homeowners that are interested in renting their home for two to three years then selling typically are facing a pain, fear, frustration, or have an ambition around selling their home or renting out their home then selling it. Just as with any business, regardless of whether they sell services or products, they all solve a problem for their customer. A chair, for example, solves your problem of needing a place to sit. A fan solves your problem of being hot and needing to cool down.

All homeowners suffer from pain, fear, and frustration, or have an ambition with respect to selling their home. It is your job to find out what it is and frame your solution as the answer to their problems.

The Pain, the Pain...

One such pain a homeowner may face is they need to relocate but if they sell their home now they will not recover their initial down payment or they will lose money. This may be as a result of payout penalties of the mortgage, high commissions to Realtors, only putting 5 percent down, not owning the home for very long, and a stagnant or a slumping housing market just to name a few.

Take, for example, one of my previous clients, a gentleman named Chang Yu. Now Chang had purchased a townhouse with three bedrooms, one-and-a-half bath, approximately 1,400 square feet, and decided that he was going to move in a couple of roommates in order to help him with the mortgage payment.

After one year, Chang had decided that he'd had enough of living with other people. Chang had also realized the home was just too big for him and he wanted to move into an apartment-style one-bedroom condo. But for Chang to turn around and sell the property, which had not gone up in value, Chang would be looking at taking a loss on the sale. He would be faced with a payout penalty on the mortgage, not getting the price he paid for the property and having to pay a Realtor about $9,000 on the sale of the home. If Chang were to go ahead with the sale he would have lost his entire 5 percent down payment and would have to pay out-of-pocket to complete the sale. This was not a position Chang wanted to be in at all.

Not only that, but the property itself was not what I would consider show-ready; it was not something that would attract many buyers. Most people are looking for something updated and this one was very much dated when it came to the kitchen, some of the flooring and the paint colours. In order to get what Chang paid for the property he would have had to invest $5,000–$10,000 into renovations. So Chang was in a position where he was motivated. He was looking for a solution that did not involve him being a landlord.

Chang contacted us because the marketing spoke directly to his pain and we had a solution that fixed his pain. So here he is in a situation where he was willing to lease out the home for three years, the duration of the majority of the mortgage term, and sell the home at the end of the term. Chang wanted a solution to his pain that wasn't going to cost him any money, didn't take up any of his time or energy and one where he could recover his initial down payment into the home.

I showed Chang how there would be no expense on his part for three years, how we would cover all the management responsibilities, pay him the carrying costs of the home for the next three years then buy it for the same price he paid for it just the year before, without any fees. Chang was ecstatic!

He saves $9,000 on Realtor fees, recovers his initial down payment, makes about $18,000 in mortgage pay-down, saves on his mortgage payout penalty, doesn't have any costs on the property for the next three years and doesn't have to do a thing. Instead of losing money, Chang is going to net an additional $30,000 over selling his home today.

Can you see how we framed our solution around Chang's pain? That is the key when you are talking with the homeowner.

I'm Afraid – I'm Very, Very Afraid!

Fear is one of the most powerful motivators that steers a lot of the decisions people make. The main fear people like Chang, who can't sell their home for financial reasons, is the fear of renting it out to tenants. Everyone has heard countless horror stories around less-than-desirable tenants. And if you have been in the investing business for any length of time, you probably have some of your own.

For the homeowners who need to rent out their home but don't want to deal with tenants or are leery about having tenants in their home, we put the emphasis more on the guarantees our company offers and, when we do our presentation, really focus in on all the expenses a homeowner would incur and the work they would need to do if they were to rent out the home themselves.

I'm going to talk more about what and how to present to the homeowner in a later chapter, but for now just know that all our presentations are exactly the same. We just emphasize the pains, fears, frustrations or ambitions the homeowner has indicated to us for the reason they called.

Usually the biggest fears homeowners have about renting are vacancy, non-payment of rent, damage to the property and constant calls to fix things. Because we already know what the fears are, we address them to the homeowner in all of our marketing material so they know exactly what they will receive. Notice I said what they receive versus what we offer.

People don't care what you do, people only care about "What's In It For Me" (WIIFM). That means in your messaging you wouldn't say "I do this" or "I do that," but rather "You receive this" and "You receive that." It is such a subtle change but one that is very powerful to your reader or listener. By informing the homeowner about all the things they receive, especially when they have indicated to you what their fears are, then there is a good chance they are saying to themselves, "This is exactly what I've been looking for" and you have a better chance of getting the homeowner to a YES.

I'm frustrated to HELL! Get me outta here!

When people get frustrated they start searching out solutions or alternatives to what they are currently doing in order to alleviate their frustration. One prime example of that is when a homeowner has had their home on the market for an extended period of time and they aren't getting many showings or offers. Often the Realtor will get the homeowner to drop their price to drive more traffic, but sometimes that just doesn't work.

When those homeowners get frustrated, you want them to know you have a solution that can alleviate their frustration. It may not be the optimal solution of paying them what they want right then and there for their house, but it is a solution where you can help them immediately and, as a side benefit, they can make up to an extra $60,000 by working with you than if they just sold their home immediately.

One of my clients – her name is Bola – had her property up for sale for approximately six months. Her husband is a doctor and at the time they were getting transferred to North Battleford, Saskatchewan, so they needed to sell the home because they were moving out of Edmonton. Prior to the transfer they put the home up for sale and got nothing. Very little traffic viewed the home and they received no offers during the six-month contract with the Realtor. Now, it was time for them to actually relocate and they still owned the house. The house was fairly priced and it was in a great neighborhood so I'm not exactly sure why the home wasn't selling.

Bola and her husband were really frustrated with the Realtor and with the situation they were in so when Bola found out about our program, she decided that it was a great fit. Since they had no desire to be distant landlords, the idea of leasing the property to our company and giving us the option to purchase was perfect. Dealing with everything, the guarantees and her getting her asking price without having to pay Realtor fees all worked well in her situation.

It was their frustrations that led them to seek out an alternative solution and contact me to explain how it worked. It was the benefits they would receive from the model that would solidify the deal. For Bola and her husband, it was a great situation and it worked extremely well. When the smoke had cleared after the three years, they had spent $0 on her home during that time and netted over $60,000 more by working with me than they would have if she had managed to sell their home back then or just rented it out and sold in the future.

Blond Ambition... Er, Actually, Hair Colour Doesn't Matter

The last and final reason people will be motivated or attracted to working with you and your solution is their desire or ambition. Their desire or ambition to make more money on the sale of the home will generally overshadow any of their pains, fears or frustrations. So one thing you will want to do when marketing to homeowners is include information to let the homeowner know they can make more money working with you than with any other method of selling their house.

I generally put in my marketing that the homeowner can make up to $60,000 more by renting their home for three years then selling. This really catches the attention of people who desire to make more money and they will generally want to find out how. In order to find out how, they book an appointment where I go and present my solution.

What I have discovered is that even through the homeowner wants to make more money, and most of them do, there are still some other pains, fears or frustrations they may have. It is important when you are marketing to the homeowners that you include information that covers all the items I have talked about in this chapter.

Many of the messages, even though they may touch on a different chord for different homeowners are all linked together and can have a very powerful impact on your ideal target market.

Action Step:

List the pains, fears, frustrations and ambitions homeowners may have when it comes to selling their home. Now, think about your solution and try to frame your solution so it addresses their pains, fears, frustrations and ambitions. Remember the WIIFM attitude. Don't tell them what you can do for them, but tell them what they receive and make sure it directly addresses their pains, fears, frustrations or ambitions.

Example: I don't want to deal with the phone calls from tenants at all hours of the night when something needs fixing.
Solution: Your property is professionally managed so any concerns or repairs the tenants require are looked after for you.

List as many as you can and then frame your solution around the problem.

To get FREE updates to this book, along with the accompanying videos, resources and materials referenced that will allow you to create your very own automated "SILVER BULLET" to help you control millions in real estate and generate a 6-figure yearly income

visit www.InfiniteRealEstateRoi.com

OR text your name and email to (587) 800-1551

OR Scan the QR Code

Chapter 6

CREATING YOUR MESSAGE

Keep Your Message Consistent

From the previous chapter you should have a good understanding of who your ideal target market is, their pains, fears, frustrations and ambitions, and how you frame your solution to solve their problems. Now it's time to start crafting your marketing message.

Copywriting is a topic that has filled volumes of books, and there is a great deal to know and understand. I'm not a copywriting expert, nor do I claim to be, but I have studied other people's work for the past five years and can get by. The next two chapters will focus on helping you create your story and craft your message.

In the last chapter you worked on framing your solution around the problems of the homeowner. Now we are going to get into creating your hook and your story. The hook is your main promise to the homeowner or what you are offering them. Your story is a quick and easy way for the homeowners to relate to you, like you and trust you.

Creating Your Hook and Your Story

When it comes to crafting your message to the homeowner there is one specific outcome that you are looking for. You want your personal story to be the vehicle for relating to and connecting with your ideal target market. You want them to get to know, like and trust you. And you also want to inspire them to take an action. For you, that action is to visit your website, opt in then sign up for a free consultation or presentation.

The story you craft is your primary vehicle for relating to and connecting with the homeowners and, again, getting them to know, like and trust you. When you are writing your story you should try to picture "the one" or your "avatar." That means try to picture your ideal homeowner, what they are going through, their age, relationship status, what's going on in their life that has led them to contact you and write your story as if you were writing to him or her.

When you are working on your story think about what it is you want to be known for because your story needs to tie back to this theme. If you want to be known for being the person who gets homeowners more money on the sale of their home, then be sure this is tied in to your story and in the message or copy you create for the homeowner. Make sure the story has a clear structure but be sure to use emotional events as connection points. Nothing gets people to take action more than having them feel or think about emotional situations.

The goal of having a personal story is to attract your ideal homeowner and repel anyone who is not. Now, a lot of people struggle with the notion that you'd want to repel anyone from doing business with you, yet in reality, you'll have much better, faster results if you target only your ideal homeowners and set yourself up to work with just the exact, right people.

The power of a compelling, connected, well-crafted, and well-delivered story is that it's a shortcut to finding and attracting your ideal homeowner. Even with all the advances in technology, the fastest way to deliver your message to your desired homeowner is still through the power of story.

Your story creates an immediate connection, emotion and desire in the homeowner to want to work with you. It gives them hope that your solution will take away their pains, fears, and frustrations and help them achieve their ambitions.

Key Principles of Crafting Your Story:

1. Decide on a message or theme, and use this as your primary framework for the story.

2. Talk to "the one." Write your story for your perfect homeowner and then practice delivering it as if you're only talking to him or her.

3. Make sure you have a clear structure, but use emotional events as connection points.

4. You want your audience to embody your story; your goal is for them to connect so deeply they ultimately want to make your story their own. The key to doing this is to make sure every point in your story is ultimately about THEM. Even when you're talking about yourself and your past experiences, you're doing so in a way that relates to and resonates with them.

5. Start as late as possible when telling your story. Instead of starting at the beginning, ask yourself, what is the latest point you can enter the story and still have it make sense?

6. Consider tense. The most effective stories are often told in the present tense, as if it's happening and unfolding in the moment.

7. Use dialogue when appropriate (especially when telling your story to an audience). It engages your audience and helps bring the characters to life.

8. Paint a picture for your audience. Use descriptive words and sensory details when possible to bring the story to life.

Exercise to Create Your Hook and Story

To help you craft your hook and story for your marketing material, website, social sites and emails, there is a worksheet included in the online resources for this book. To access the worksheets visit www.InfiniteRealEstateRoi.com

Here are some of the key questions to answer that will help you craft your story or message to the home owners.

1. What do you want to be known for? What is the ideal or core promise that you represent to the homeowners? What is it the homeowners aspire to have or do that you

can reflect back to them?

2. What are the top three to five biggest pains, fears, and frustrations of your ideal homeowner?

3. List as many of the primary objections and concerns your ideal homeowner may have about doing business with you. How can you help them overcome those objections?

4. What are the key moments in a homeowner's life where they went through a significant transformation that you helped them get from where they were to where they are today? What can you share from this that will connect to the homeowners you are going to be talking with? The best stories are those based on real-life events that had a great deal of emotion around them.

5. Based on your answers to the above questions, what is your core message or theme? If there were two sentences that summarized what you are about and how you can help the homeowners, what would they be?

6. What are the main points you want to make

in your story that will back this theme up? What are your sub-points that will continue to connect the homeowners back to your core message and theme?

7. Write out a structured outline for your personal narrative or story. Make sure you have a beginning, a middle and an end. Use this format:
    a. Opening hook: you have to start strong and draw the reader or listener into your story.
    b. Core promise: make sure your audience knows there will be a payoff from the story that directly relates to them.
    c. Your personal pain points (from the past): be as descriptive and vulnerable as possible.
    d. The defining moment where you had a breakthrough: the moment you had a realization or new thought or new idea that broke you out of your pain and to the next level of what it is you were looking for.
    e. Paint a picture of what your life is like today (make this aspirational; something your target market aspires to have, be, share, give or do).

Going through this type of exercise is very important and will be used when writing the copy for your website, flyers, ads and the emails you send out to the homeowners.

Effective Copy

Now it's time to bring together all the information you worked on in the last chapter and so far in this chapter into the actual copy you will need to use in your flyers, websites, social media and emails you send out to the clients.

There are three critical things you will require to create compelling copy. Without these three critical things it is impossible to create compelling copy that will really work well.

The first thing you need is to have clarity of the outcome. Before you start writing about anything, you need to be crystal clear on what you want the outcome to be. What is the goal of the copy and how will you know if you have achieved it? You must always start with the end in mind. The end, in your case, is to have the homeowner contact you to arrange for a free consultation or presentation by you on how your solution will alleviate their pains, fears, and frustrations or achieve their ambition.

The second thing that is critical for your copy to be compelling is to have full clarity of who your audience is and understand their pains, fears, frustrations and ambitions so you can craft your message accordingly. We have spent the past two chapters ensuring you are completely clear on this component.

The third and final component to ensure you are creating compelling copy is to have full clarity of your value in the equation. You must be clear on what value you bring to the table and why the homeowner should pay attention to you and what you have to say. This is where you connect the dots between something the homeowner wants and the outcome you want to achieve, which is to lease-option their house.

Keys to Effective Copywriting

Now that you have lined up your three critical elements to creating compelling copy, it is time to get into actually writing the effective copy that will get the homeowner to contact you for a presentation on the solution. These are very powerful components when you are creating copy intended to generate a result. Many of these are powerful mental triggers that build on each other.

1. Get their Attention: It is imperative that you

get the homeowner's attention right from the very start. This is the most important part of your copy because it has to pull them in and make them want to keep reading. The headline or title should be clear and easily understood immediately. Some of the things you can do in your title to grab attention is to build curiosity, ask them a question, use controversy or identify a specific audience.

2. Identify the Problem: You quickly need to identify the problem the homeowner is facing because the rest of the copy is built on this problem and your solution. If the homeowner can't identify with the problem they won't want more information about your solution.

3. Show them the Solution: Here is where you show them what they need and how you're going to make their problem go away or help them get what they want.

4. Focus on the Benefits: This is absolutely critical and goes along with the solution. This is where you focus on the benefits the homeowner will receive, not the features of your solution.

5. Present the Offer: Here is where you tell them specifically about what you're offering. Lay out exactly what they get when they move forward. Make it as real and tangible as possible by showing images if you can.

6. Show your Credibility: This is about your story of authority and your right to offer the solution. If you are just getting started it is good to partner with someone who has the credibility.

7. Provide them with Social Proof: If you have any testimonials, references, known authorities, proof of others that have tried it, or success stories with other people talking about your solution it will be more believable.

8. Remove the Risk: People want to know it is low to no risk on their part. They are looking for guarantees and want to be sure there is no downside should they move forward. Make it clear to them it is a free no-pressure consultation. You are there to present them with the option and educate them on your solution.

9. Create a sense of Urgency: You need them

to make a decision right now, so you will want to place a sense of urgency on your offer. Authentic scarcity is one of the most powerful urgency triggers. You need them to understand why they need to make a decision now and what happens if they don't. One thing you can indicate is that you are only accepting a few homes in their area into your program; once your quota is filled you won't be accepting any more.

10. Call to Action: Here you want to be very clear on what you want them to do. After they have gone through the information or video you want them to fill in the form to book their free no-pressure consultation. You may want to even repeat exactly what the action is you want them to take.

11. Consequence for not taking Action: What happens if they don't take action? How worse off will they be if they don't solve their problem? What has happened to others that didn't solve their problem?

12. Summarize important Points: This is where you summarize the most important points and repeat the urgency. This is the P.S. to your entire offer so it needs to be compelling and standalone.

By working through all 12 components of effective copywriting, combined with the exercise to create your hook and your story, you should now have enough material to create the copy for your websites, create flyers, and create ads as well as emails for your follow-up sequence.

Now, it's time to build the system.

To get FREE updates to this book, along with the accompanying videos, resources and materials referenced that will allow you to create your very own automated "SILVER BULLET" to help you control millions in real estate and generate a 6-figure yearly income

visit www.InfiniteRealEstateRoi.com

OR text your name and email to (587) 800-1551

OR Scan the QR Code

Section 2: The System

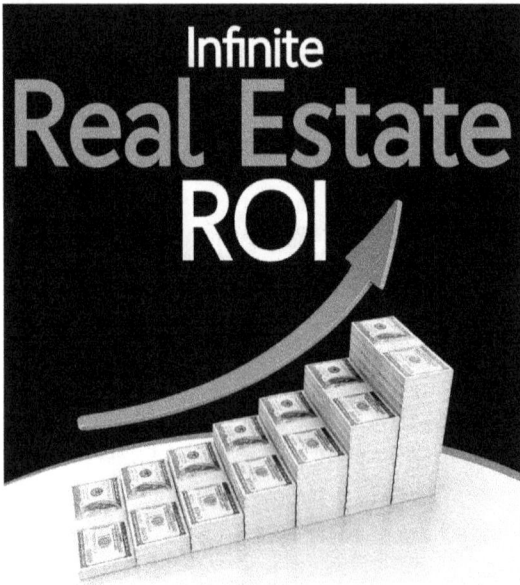

John A. McCabe

Chapter 7

GENERATING TRAFFIC

Now that you have spent some time and energy crafting the message, it's time to show you where and how it will be used by getting into the components that make up the system that will generate your leads and opportunities.

I find the easiest way to understand what it is you need to build is to create a visual diagram of the flow of how the system works. The diagram I am going to reference is located in the online resources for this book at www.InfiniteRealEstateROI.com. It is called the Infinite Real Estate ROI Flow Diagram.

The major components that make up the system include the following:

1. Generated Traffic – from sources such as:
   f. Social media
   g. Flyers
   h. Ads
   i. Searches
2. Lead Capture Site – containing:
   a. Compelling video to get them to opt

     in
  b. Opt-in form for lead-capture (name and email)
  c. Compelling copy as to why the should give you their name and email
  d. Ethical bribe – FREE giveaway in exchange for name and email
  e. Thank-you page containing video and free giveaway
  f. Appointment booking form to turn lead into opportunity
3. Autoresponder System
  a. Captures the leads
  b. Automatically sends a series of emails until unsubscribe or book appt
  c. Converts leads to opportunities when appointment is booked
  d. Sends automatic response when requesting appointment
4. Presentation material for meeting the homeowner
  a. Example of renting a home
  b. Example of selling a home
  c. Example of renting three years vs. rent-to-own vs. working with you
  d. Blank forms for running numbers on their house

Generating Traffic

This is where everything starts: traffic generation. The goal of this system is to generate as much traffic as possible to your lead-capture page, more commonly known as a squeeze page, where you want the homeowner to enter their name and email address. In many circles this is called building your list. List-building is one of the core strategies in any successful business today.

So what do I mean by list? This is really simple – it's a list of people who have asked for more information or to receive emails from you. This is done through an opt-in form on your website or squeeze page, and people enter their name and email to get access to your free stuff and receive your emails.

So before we get too far into the specifics as to why someone would give you their name and email, we need to get the people to your website or squeeze page first. There are a variety of ways this can be done but we are going to focus on just a few of the key strategies.

Flyers

This may seem low-tech but it is still very effective when you add in some new strategies for capturing people's information. The message on the flyer needs to be very clear and follow much of what you went through in the chapter on creating your message. Remember, grab their attention with the title or headline, speak to the "one" and address what pains, fears, frustrations or ambitions your solution is going to solve for them. Also, if you recall, make sure you frame your solution around their issues. The old "what's in it for me" comes up because you need to keep your ideal target's issues in the forefront of your mind.

Here are some things to keep in mind when you are creating the copy for your flyer. Keep in mind, your flyer is an extension of your squeeze page, and as such should use the same verbiage or copy.

✓ Make the title of the flyer short and to the point. It should be a few words and be your main hook or your promise to the homeowner.

✓ The title should also be clear and easily understood… instantly.

✓ The subtitle needs to explain clearly what the flyer is about (a short but compelling promise).

✓ Use the art of description – paint a clear picture with words

✓ Your goal – attract attention and create interest

✓ Be specific – your title and subtitle should offer a clear solution to be aimed at a tightly focused, highly targeted audience.

✓ Be conversational – avoid big words

Here are some great questions to ask yourself as you are crafting the title, subtitle and the copy for the flyer.

✓ What is your clear promise?

✓ What is the primary problem are you solving for the homeowner?

✓ Why would someone want to have you come give them a presentation?

✓ What would the homeowner type into Google (or another search engine) when looking for solutions to their problems?

✓ What is the format of the solution you're providing: A formula? A blueprint? A system? A lifestyle? A philosophy? An automated tool?

When you have crafted the message you are going to use on your flyer, make sure it is consistent with the message throughout your entire system.

Something to keep in mind is the more methods you provide to the homeowner for opting in to your campaign or getting access to the free information or "ethical bribe", the more leads you will get. Most people only put the website address on the flyer, but if you include a telephone number they can call and leave a message with their name and email, the same number where they can just text their name and email address, and a QR code that takes them to the opt-in page automatically, then the number of leads you capture will dramatically increase.

It is important to have all methods of capturing leads funnel into one single autoresponder campaign that is set to follow up automatically with text messages and emails. Since around half the people access the Internet using their mobile device, it is important to be able to send the video or the report directly to their phone. Visit www.InfiniteRealEstateRoi.com to get information on the system I use that will allow you to capture leads all these different ways.

These flyers are typically given out at trade shows, networking events or delivered to houses in specific neighborhoods. You can contract services like the postal service or flyer services to specifically target neighborhoods you are looking to lease-option properties. Targeting neighborhoods where your qualified tenant buyers want property is a great way to close on rent-to-own deals very quickly.

Ads

Online classifieds are a great way to drive traffic to your lead-capture page. People are specifically advertising and looking in the ads located on sites like Kijiji.ca, CraigsList.com, and eBayClassifieds.com for selling and renting their houses. By placing an ad on the most common sites for your area, you will help generate more traffic.

The ad used for online classifieds should contain the same title or heading as your flyer, as well as most of the body of the ad. You should also include all the same opt-in methods as the flyer, such as website, phone, text and QR code. Kijiji ads have been very good to me over the past five years. I have received a lot of leads from Kijiji that are interested in my services.

You can also look at placing paid ads in Google or Facebook. I talk about these types of ads in the Social Media section.

Internet Searches

Positioning yourself to be where your ideal customers are looking for help can be an easy way to generate traffic. The best way to do that is to research some possible keyword phrases that homeowners in your area may be entering into search engines like Google. To determine what people may be looking for, use the Google Keyword Tool (type in Google Keyword Tool in Google to access) and start entering things people may be searching for.

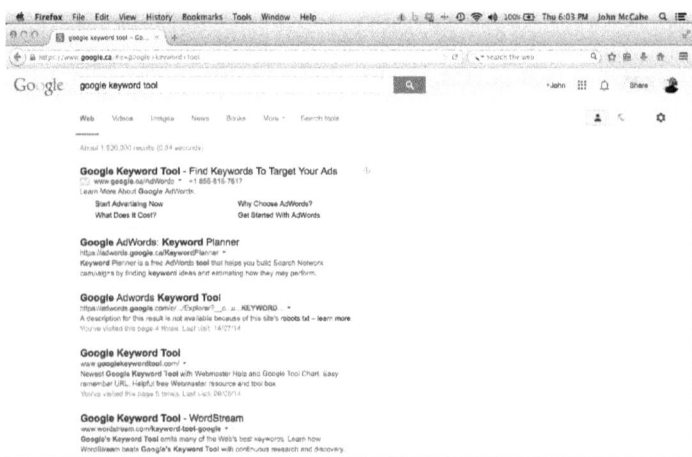

Here are a few suggested searches you can try to see if you get any results.

- ✓ How to sell your house
- ✓ How to sell a house
- ✓ Sell your house fast

- ✓ Sell my house fast
- ✓ Selling a house

It is important you find one or two keyword phrases and use those phrases whenever you are putting content on the Internet. Even in your ads on Kijiji, for example, you will want to try and fit the specific phrase in the title and several times in the body of the ad.

It is also important you register a domain name with the keywords in the url. For example, if "how to sell your house" was the phrase you wanted to focus on and use then you would want to put that in the url of your website, along with your city name. So for me I would want to see if I could register the domain www.HowToSellYourHouseInEdmonton.com. I quickly just went to check and the domain is available. Maybe I better buy it before this book comes out.

You will also want to put your url in all of your posts as well, since it contains your keyword phrase, which gives you another instance for using your phrase in the same post. The more times you can use the phrase in the post, as long as it makes sense, the better. Just don't fill your post full of the phrase if it doesn't read naturally.

This comes into play in the next section when I talk about social media and content.

Social Media and Content

In today's Internet world the new SEO (Search Engine Optimization) is all about content and engagement. Putting out content to the big social media players, including Facebook, Twitter, YouTube and LinkedIn, will help you create what is called organic traffic. Organic traffic is when people go to your website because they click on some of the content you have placed on the Internet, versus paid traffic such as Google ads and Facebook ads.

For Facebook I highly recommend something called a **DARK POST**. It is a way you can create a sponsored ad that does not show up on your Facebook wall. Let's face it; making the same post over and over will just make your friends and followers angry. But if you do a dark post, which doesn't show up on your wall but gives you the ability to drill down and be very specific as to who gets to see it, can be very beneficial.

You may decide you want people on Facebook in your city who specifically have been looking or searching for Realtors to sell their house. All of a sudden on their wall a post shows up that says how they can make $60,000 more working with you than with a Realtor. They think, "Wow, what timing." But in reality you programmed the post to reach them because they were searching for Realtors.

To find out more about dark posts, do a search in YouTube for "dark post" and you will see how you set it up and create your search criteria.

When it comes to creating content on the various types of social media, they are not all created equal. I recommend a book by Gary Vaynerchuk called "Jab, Jab, Jab, Right Hook," which breaks down the various social media types and the best way to post on each site. I also recommend you create your posts in advance and set up a schedule and use a tool that automatically posts to your social media accounts at the scheduled times.

When you post to social media, be sure to use the keyword phrase you researched for Internet searches in the title of your posts as well as in the body whenever you can. This will help you get found when people are searching in Google for that phrase. Remember, social is the new SEO of the Internet. The more social content you have with the keyword phrase, the better chance you will be on the first page of Google for the search terms – especially with YouTube, since Google owns it. It isn't enough just to post – you need to get engagement from other people, so having them like or comment on your post is very important as well.

So there you have the four main methods for generating traffic to your website or squeeze page, where the exchange of contact information for value will take place. In the next chapter I will talk about the squeeze page, what you need to have on the page, the ethical bribe and the autoresponder system.

To get FREE updates to this book, along with the accompanying videos, resources and materials referenced that will allow you to create your very own automated "SILVER BULLET" to help you control millions in real estate and generate a 6-figure yearly income

visit www.InfiniteRealEstateRoi.com

**OR text your name and email to
(587) 800-1551**

OR Scan the QR Code

Chapter 8

SQUEEZE PAGE

Generating traffic is of little use without the right type of website, lead-capture page or squeeze page. Now you may be saying to yourself, "Well I already have a website and I'm not getting any leads." This is probably very true. In my opinion, there is only one purpose of a website, lead-capture page or squeeze page, and that is to get people to join your list, meaning give you their name and email.

The difference between a website and a lead or squeeze page is the number of pages. A website generally has five or more pages with a navigation bar where you can move from page to page freely. A squeeze page is a very simple single page that gives the visitor a choice of only two options:

1. The visitor can opt in with their name and email address to get your free item (this is your ethical bribe).
2. The visitor can leave the page.

By forcing the visitor to choose, you force them to

choose. You should also understand right from the beginning that for most websites the majority of visitors will choose to leave your site. For most, when they leave the site it is rare they will return, even if they bookmark the website. If you doubt this, just think about your own actions on the Internet. Once people leave your site, they will never think about it again, unless you capture their email address. Everything changes if they join your list because then you can send messages to their email to drive them back to your website, or any other site, for that matter.

You can have a squeeze page as your landing page as well. This means you have a regular website with five-plus pages but when someone comes to your site, the first thing they encounter is a squeeze page, so the only way they can gain access to the information on your website is by entering their email address. If they don't, then they don't get to see what is on your website. If they do give their email address then they can access the info and will not encounter the squeeze page should they come back to the site.

When you think of your website as a list-building machine, it starts to make a lot more sense to put up a squeeze page and force people to make a choice when they come to your site. Make them either opt in or leave.

Your Squeeze Page Formula

There are seven components that go into having a successful squeeze page.

1. Simple and visually appealing design. You want to make sure your squeeze page has inviting colors and compelling graphics. Things like photos, logos, any relevant images, arrows and buttons are all part of a good-quality successful squeeze page.

2. Strong attention-getting headline. We spoke about this in the earlier chapter on writing and creating good, compelling copy. Remember to keep in mind the "what's in it for me?" question when you are creating the headline. Again, it always boils down to their pains, fears, frustrations and ambitions.

3. Irresistible ethical bribe, which is considered your free giveaway. The bribe should clearly address the homeowner's pains, fears, frustrations or ambitions. Things you can use for an ethical bribe include:
   a.   Special report

  b. E-book

  c. E-course

  d. Video series

  e. Audio interview series

  f. Webinar (live or automated)

4. A short video. This video should be kept to two or three minutes in length, be full motion (you) or screen capture (voice over a slide show). Again, the script needs to stick close to the rest of the copy and address the pains, fears, frustrations or ambitions of the homeowner. It needs to introduce and talk about the ethical bribe and tell them what their call to action should be, which is to enter their name and email in the form on the page.

5. Relevant bolded and bulleted copy. These will typically address the pains, fears, frustrations or ambitions, provide solutions for the homeowner and summarize some of the key points in the video.

6. Visible signup form and submit button. You want to make sure the instructions are simple and clear. Use a button with a good call to action and a contrasting colour such as blue, yellow or red. Avoid boring calls to action like "sign up here" or "submit."

Instead, use things like "Get FREE Access," or "Send me FREE Report!"

7. Include a privacy statement below the submit button. This will let people know that you value their privacy and will not share their contact info with anyone.

When someone opts in to your squeeze page it will take him or her to a confirmation or thank-you page. On this page make sure you offer them thanks for their subscription, provide them simple next steps for receiving their ethical bribe via email, offer them further instructions on steps to take if they do not receive the email and provide a link or email for the help desk.

Ethical Bribe

The strength of your ethical bribe will determine if people are going to take that next step and contact you for a consultation. The exercise you went through in crafting your hook and your story will be a lot of the copy for your ethical bribe.

Remember, the bribe can take many forms, such as a special report, an E-book, an E-course, video or audio series and live or automated webinars. Regardless of the form it takes the structure should be very much in line with point 7 in the exercise to create your hook and story. If you recall the structure went like this:

Write out a structured outline for your personal narrative or story. Make sure you have a beginning, middle and an end. Use this format:

(1) Opening hook: you have to start strong and draw the reader or listener into your story.

(2) Core promise: make sure your audience knows there will be a payoff from the story that directly relates to them.

(3) Your personal pain points (from the past): be as descriptive and vulnerable as possible.

(4) The defining moment where you had a breakthrough: the moment you had a realization or new thought or new idea that broke you out of your pain and to the next level of what it is you were looking for.

(5) Paint a picture of what your life is like today (make this aspirational; something your target market aspires to have, be, share, give or do).

(6) Tell them what action you want them to take

You will want to use this structure and bring in as many emotional components and transformational stories of people you have helped who are just like the homeowner reading this report or watching this video. Regardless of the form your ethical bribe takes, this format will help you create a compelling ethical bribe that will get people to take the action you want.

Autoresponder

When people enter their name and email in the form to get access to your ethical bribe, you want that form to be linked to an autoresponder. This links your form to a system that captures your subscriber's information in one database and sends out messages on your behalf. This is how you build your list.

The messages that get sent out need to be crafted and set up by you initially, but when this is done you don't need to worry about sending out anything manually. For example, when someone first enters their information you may have the system set to send out a message immediately thanking them for taking the time to get more information and a link to their FREE ethical bribe. The next day you may have a message set to be sent talking about some of the content in the video and asking them to book their FREE no-obligation consultation.

In each message you send out you want to address a specific pain, fear, frustration or ambition and show how your solution can help the homeowner achieve their desired result by working with you. Remember to word your emails so it is all about the homeowner and not about what you do. You also want to ask them to take action, which is to book their appointment with you.

Generally you have anywhere from five to seven messages set up to go out in the first two weeks, then you would move to having one message sent out per month. They will continue to get messages from you until they take one of two actions.

1.   They unsubscribe from your list, which indicates they no longer want to receive emails from you about your service.

2.   They take the action your emails encourage them to do, which is fill in a form requesting you to come give them a FREE no-obligation consultation.

As soon as they fill in the form requesting the consultation, you want to have your system set to remove them from the first list, which are the people who just opted in for your ethical bribe, and put them in a new list for the people who requested the consultation. You want to do this so the people who have committed to a consultation don't keep getting messages asking them to commit again. This way you can have a different set of messages set to follow up with the people you have presented to but not yet made the decision to lease you their property giving you the option to buy. In these messages you are discussing the pains, fears, frustrations or ambitions and how your solution can help them fix whatever problems or perceived problems they have. This keeps you in the forefront of their mind.

There is a variety of autoresponder systems available ranging from free to $199 per month or even more. The price is typically dependent on the number of features the program has, along with its versatility. A list of all the tech resources I recommend can be found in the online resources by visiting www.InfiniteRealEstateRoi.com.

Remember, the main purpose of the autoresponder is to be able to follow up with your leads and turn them into opportunities. Educating them and addressing their pains, fears, frustrations or ambitions so they will take the action you want them to take, contact you for a consultation. Once you get them to commit to the consultation, it's now time to prepare for your meeting with the homeowner and present them the solution that is going to be the answer to their pains, fears, frustrations or ambitions.

To get FREE updates to this book, along with the accompanying videos, resources and materials referenced that will allow you to create your very own automated "SILVER BULLET" to help you control millions in real estate and generate a 6-figure yearly income

visit www.InfiniteRealEstateRoi.com

OR text your name and email to (587) 800-1551

OR Scan the QR Code

Chapter 9

PRESENTING TO THE HOMEOWNER

Your system is set up and running smoothly, you are driving some great traffic to your squeeze page and they opted in for your ethical bribe. If your bribe was right on the money you should have a high percentage of people contacting you wanting a free consultation. During the consultation you show them how they will make more money working with you by putting their home into your program.

Your system should be set up so the instant someone contacts you about getting a free consultation you get an email or a text message directly to your phone with the relevant information you need to follow up. Even though you have set your system up to automatically send them an email I would have a series of interactive text messages sent to the lead as well.

By having automated interactive text messages you can gather more information from the client that will make your job easier when you actually contact them. You can have the system ask questions that are this or that questions. Things like whether they would you rather meet during the day or in the evening, asking them to provide two different days of the week that work would work best, and to provide two times during those days that work best. Basically you can have your system follow up to book the appointment for you automatically.

I would also follow up with the person via phone within the hour if possible. By having automated systems following up instantaneously and gathering information for you, plus you actually calling to confirm the appointment and gather more information about the home, you are subconsciously letting the homeowner know you are organized and you respect them as a potential customer. An MIT study has shown that people are more responsive when you follow up with them in less than five minutes. It isn't always possible to do that in person, but having a system that does it automatically with emails and text messages can go a long way for your credibility.

When you go to call the homeowner to confirm the date and time you will want to gather more information about their home. You can get a copy of a homeowner questionnaire in the resources section of the members' area. The important questions you want to ask include:

- ✓ Year built
- ✓ Square footage
- ✓ Style of property (condo, townhouse, bungalow, bi-level, split level)
- ✓ Number of bedrooms
- ✓ Number of bathrooms
- ✓ Parking? Garage? Attached/detached?
- ✓ Fireplace?
- ✓ Appliances?

For the full list of things to ask, please access the resources section by visiting www.InfiniteRealEstateRoi.com

You will need all this information prior to your visit with the homeowner as you need to do your research on their property. There are two main things you need to find out. First, what do properties like theirs rent for in their area and what do properties like theirs sell for in their area? Now keep in mind I said "sell for," not what they list for. A lot of homeowners will tell you what houses are listed for on MLS or some other website, which is really irrelevant. All that really matters is what people actually pay for the properties.

You will also want to make sure you are comparing apples to apples, so if the properties that have sold all had finished basements or garages or upgraded kitchens, while your homeowner's doesn't, then you need to adjust the estimated selling price of their home. Regardless of the condition of their home, everyone thinks they live in a castle and that it is worth way more than anyone else's in the neighborhood.

Be confident of your numbers and how you came to the calculation. You will want to be very well prepared when you go and meet with the homeowner. One thing I've done is actually prepare an example of a typical home and some examples of what the homeowner would make if they sold it today and how much they would cash flow if they were actually to rent the home today. It can be an eye-opener for most homeowners.

I also use that information to do a scenario of the homeowner renting the house out themselves or with a property management company, then selling it with a Realtor. Basically, you are going to need to compare how much they make if they did it themselves versus them working with you.

Here is a sample list of the things I go through with the homeowner with respect to renting their house.

Mortgage Payment
Taxes
Insurance
Repairs and Capital Improvements
Electricity / Hydro (if tenant pays you still have to allow for the time when it is vacant)
Gas / Heat (if tenant pays you still have to allow for the time when it is vacant)
Water / Sewer (if tenant pays you still have to allow for the time when it is vacant)
Lawn / Snow (if tenant pays you still have to allow for the time when it is vacant)
Cable / Phone (if paid by owner)
Management (if self-managed one must consider the cost of their time)
Advertising
Pest Control
Security (Change all the locks or locksmith)
Trash Removal (if not included in the taxes and not paid by tenant)
Bad Debts (tenant is in the property and not paying)
Eviction Costs (hiring a bailiff or lawyer)
Accountant – Renting is a business
Other

When it comes to the topic of repairs and maintenance here is a list of a few things I would discuss with the homeowner and get them to give me some figures as to how much they think it would cost when a tenant moves out of the home.

Painting
Flooring
Roof
Furnace Cleaning
Trades – Electrician / Plumber / Carpenter
Exterior Maintenance
Hot Water Tank
Other

When it comes to selling their house we want to make sure they factor things in like the percent of the asking price they would get, commissions, how long it sits on the market as well as the length of time it takes to close on the sale. Here is a list that I use in my presentation with the homeowner.

Getting the Property Show-Ready
Loss of Income During the Sale Period (5m)
Realtor Fees
Advertising Costs (if not using a Realtor)
Legal / Closing Costs

Generally when you are walking the homeowner through the lists you want to elicit their opinion of the values. It becomes very hard for the homeowner to dispute the numbers when they have come up with the values themselves. Of course, your example has already been filled in by what you consider to be industry standards based on what you know and have been taught.

It is important to compare them renting the home for three years then selling the home, and working with you. For them to rent for three years they are going to have turnover of tenants, vacancy, repairs, etc. When you are going through your example you want to get them to see that what they are actually going to net in the end is way less then they expected. For most people they only think in terms of gross figures and don't actually think of the true expenses involved and the resulting net figure.

When you have actually worked through the entire three years, even with the home being appreciated during those three years, they still end up with far less than they actually would have ever imagined. It is important, and your role, to guide them down the path of understanding the reality of the situation. This is the key to getting them to say "yes" at the end of the presentation.

My offer to the homeowner has become a formula, which I'm going to share with you. I offer them today's fair market value of their home, less a $200-per-month management fee that comes off the price at the end if and only if I buy the home. I also offer them fair market rent less $200 per month, so if fair market rent is $2,000 I will offer them $1,800. I also offer to pay guaranteed if it is vacant or filled and look after all the repairs and maintenance under $1,000 per repair. You can find out more about the specifics of how I structure my rent-to-owns by getting a copy of my book "Rent To Own Revolution" at www.RentToOwnRevolution/book.

It is important they understand that working with you is a far better and more lucrative and stress-free option than doing it on their own, even if they use property managers and Realtors.

One thing I want to address is that when I'm going through the presentation with the homeowner and I ask them about situations to get a number for a line item and they come back with something way off-base or unrealistic, and it becomes a regular thing with each line item, then I will actually stop. I will stop the presentation and I will start to "close up shop," meaning start making gestures like putting the cap on my pen, bringing my papers together as if I'm getting ready to go and just telling the homeowner I don't think this program is for them.

They just don't have a true grasp of what it takes to sell or rent out a home, they are very unrealistic with respect to their numbers, and because of that I'm not interested in wasting any more of my time.

This will go one of two ways: they agree and you leave, or they say, "No, no, no, you are right." You see, this is not a hard sell, this is not about convincing anyone – this is about educating the homeowner on the reality of the situation based on years of experience in this business. If they don't value your expertise or your opinion, then don't waste your time. This is where it helps to be recognized as the trusted authority in your marketplace. Don't be afraid to walk away from the presentation if the homeowner is being unrealistic.

One advantage my private coaching clients and certified consultants have over most investors trying to do this business is they get to take advantage of the credibility and authority I've built over the past five years. The quickest way to establishing authority is to write a number one best-seller, which "Rent To Own Revolution" reached when it was released. They also get a complete package of material they can use and take with them to meet with the homeowners. It includes an actual example, blank forms for calculating the homeowner's home, and scripts for walking the homeowner through the presentation, including what to say in various situations. This makes their presentations and negotiations go a lot smoother.

When I first started it took me 20–25 presentations over the course of a month before I got my first yes. Now, with the system I have built and developed I am closing anywhere from 50-75% of the home owners I'm presenting to. If I meet with 20 then I know if I use the presentation system I've developed and just follow the steps, the scripts and the materials then I can close between 10-15 of the homeowners.

If you use the information in this chapter to create a presentation you will be light years ahead of where I was, right out of the gate. The one thing I didn't do was give up, and neither should you. I knew if there were that many people contacting me about my solution, then they were interested – I just had to figure out how to present it to them. It took me a long time and several meetings with my coach and mentor before I was able to put together the presentation I currently use and give to my private coaching clients and certified consultants.

The system you created will get your foot in the door but continuously working on your presentation and always wanting it to get better will enable you to close deals. I have uploaded an audio file of a mock presentation between my coach, Ross, who plays the investor, and myself, who plays the homeowner. You will actually get to hear a master of NLP and negotiating walk through the presentation with the homeowner and react to questions or comments I make. I've also added the transcribed notes from the audio file so you can read them as well. Be sure to go to www.InfiniteRealEstateRoi.com to access the information. It will be a great resource to help you build your presentation when meeting the homeowner.

At this point in time, you should have walked the homeowner through an example of how much they would make if they sold today, how much they would make if they just turned it into a rental, and how much they would make by renting it out for 3 years then selling it themselves. The last one you compared against you leasing the home from them and offering to buy it at the end of the term. There should be a large difference between what they make working with you versus doing it themselves.

After you have gone through the example home you have prepared in advance, it is time to see if the homeowner is interested. You now ask them what their thoughts are and if they see how this could work for their home. If they don't agree at this point it is better to work with you then there isn't much sense in going through the numbers on their home. If they get it and see the advantage of working with you and how you can eliminate their pains, fears, frustrations or get them to their ambition then now is the time to go through the information for their home. This is a great sign that they are very interested and where you work on the close.

When you have gone through the information on their home there may be some negotiations with respect to your offer, so know what your upper and lower limits are for their home. Have a range for your lease amount and your purchase amount, and stay within your range. You should have calculated this prior to coming to the meeting when you are analyzing the sandwich lease option numbers for their home.

When they say, "YES" then make an appointment right then to get together and go over the contracts.

Congratulations! You just signed your first lease option home.

To get FREE updates to this book, along with the accompanying videos, resources and materials referenced that will allow you to create your very own automated "SILVER BULLET" to help you control millions in real estate and generate a 6-figure yearly income

visit www.InfiniteRealEstateRoi.com

OR text your name and email to (587) 800-1551

OR Scan the QR Code

Chapter 10

WHAT'S NEXT

At this point you are asking yourself, "What do I do with this?"

Easy. Just do it.

Like anything in life that matters, it requires a little preparation and implementation.

This book, like many others, has a great number of actionable items. If you take the information and actionable items and start to implement them you will be well on your way to creating a system that will generate you more leads and opportunities then you will be able to handle.

However, it has been my experience that probably 97-98% of the people who read this book will do absolutely nothing. Not that they don't see the benefits of the system but they just get overwhelmed and let the tech get in their way.

It is more important you understand the flow of the information and how it should work. The tech part of the system is a commodity, meaning you can outsource that part of your system relatively inexpensively. Websites like Odesk.com, fiverr.com, elance.com etc have made it easier to get work done relatively inexpensively.

One of the most important parts of the entire system is your copy. It will be what you put on your website, what you have as your ethical bribe, what you put in your autoresponder emails and what you have in your presentation. These things have taken my 5 years an investment of almost $50,000 into marketing courses, coaching and masterminds to get them to where they are today. Getting it right has given me a return 10x's my investment just in one year. Remember, each homeowner YES is worth $50,000-$60,000 and you only need to 2-3 per year to make $10,000 per month or more. Even if this system helped you close one homeowner per year, it is well worth the investment.

The great news is I've created some complete done for you systems that combines various aspects of this book. Everything from copy for your website, a done for your system all set and ready to go right to being a Certified Rent To Own Revolution Consultant where you get the benefit of my materials, experience, authority and brand to enhance and grow your real estate investing business either part-time or full-time.

Sample Package

I realize that copy writing is the most crucial piece of the equation for most of you. Because of this, one of the packages I'm making available to those investors interested in making the investment into creating a system where they can generate an abundance of leads and opportunities.

This package will contain the following:
- ✓ A sample of my flyer – You will receive the actual flyer I use and hand out to homeowners. You will see the layout of the flyer as well as the copy I use to attract the attention of the homeowner. You will also see how I use the multiple opt-in methods to increase the number of people who I get to want access to my Ethical Bribe.

- ✓ Ethical Bribe – You receive the script I used to create the video I use as my ethical bribe. There is some great copy within the script and it touches on the pains, fears, frustrations, and ambitions of the homeowners and uses some key wording and phrasing to get them to take action. This would be a great framework for you to build your very own script for a video or use aspects of it as a base for your FREE report.

- ✓ The copy I use on my squeeze page. – This copy is in line with the copy on the flyer as well as the ethical bribe. Everything must be congruent in order for the message to remain consistent. You will also receive a snap shot of the squeeze page so you get an idea how to incorporate the elements discussed in the book. You will also receive a screen shot of the Thank You page as well.

- ✓ Autoresponder sequence – You will receive the copy for the 7 emails in the email sequence as well as when the emails are set to be delivered to the homeowner.

- ✓ Homeowner Presentation Package – For the very first time I am making the presentation I use to get the homeowners to say yes, along with a script, available to people outside my private coaching clients and certified consultants. You can use the presentation as a starting point and model your own presentation with the information in this package.

- ✓ Tech and outsourcers – You will receive the names of the exact tech I use to run my entire system. You will also receive the contact information of some of the individuals I use when I outsource some of my work.

This package is perfect for the tech savvy individual who just may need some help with the copy writing aspect. For you, setting up the system is second nature, but you are stumped at the wording and how to present to the homeowner. This package will give you a great starting point that you can model and even take some of the information to use for your own purposes.

Obviously I use my own stories in my examples and have everything branded for my company. You will need to create your own copy and use your own brand in everything you do. Access to the information does not constitute authorization to use my brand or any of the copy written materials for your own use. It is meant to be a guide and model for creating your own system.

Done For You System

For many of you reading this book, I realize that even having examples of the copy you can model, the systems I use, and the outsourcers I use is still not enough to get you started. For you, I wanted to put together a complete package from A-Z that is completely turn key.

Once you take delivery of the complete done for you system you have everything you need to get started. All you need to do is use the tools provided to start driving traffic to your lead generating site and book consultations with the homeowner. Everything discussed in the Sample Package will be set up and designed for you and your brand. Everything will have your brand, your contact information and ready to go. The ethical bribe will include a screen capture video, voice over slide show, designed to be congruent with the overall message and to drive the homeowner to take action and book a consultation with you.

You also get a complete branded package, and script, to use when meeting the homeowner. You will have a package to give the homeowner and your own version with specific scripts and prompting questions to help you walk through the presentation and get the homeowner to the point of saying YES.

This program is ideal for the investor who wants to get started right away. You don't want to figure out what to write, how to build the system from scratch and build a presentation to meet the homeowner. You just want to hit the ground running and make some things happen FAST! This package will enable you to do that without worrying about any of the set up.

Certified Rent To Own Revolution Consultant

For some, you may be just starting out, unsure of what you are doing or just want to be part of a proven model and brand. You want to be part of a brand that has recognition, is a trusted authority in the marketplace, operates with the true win-win-win philosophy and is there to support and help each consultant grow his or her investment business.

How do you think it would help you in your business if I gave you full access to my model, brand, credibility, authority and my support? How quickly would your business grow if I was helping convince the homeowners to contact you for a consultation, then after the consultation helping get them to say YES to leasing their home to you.

What would it do for your business if I helped qualify all your tenant buyers and set them up for success? If I gave you access to my personal mortgage broker and credit coach to deal with all your tenant buyer prospects?

What about giving you unlimited access to get all your questions answered? Having access to a monthly live cast coaching session? What if you never had to worry about keeping up with technology changes or the best ways to get people into your lead funnel? What about having someone else submitting content to various websites on a monthly basis to increase your Google rankings and be where your ideal clients are looking and being able to drive them to your websites?

As a certified consultant you get the following:
- ✓ Complete Rent To Own Revolution Branded lead generating system for homeowners.

- ✓ Complete presentation package when meeting the homeowner.

- ✓ Full tenant buyer website designed to rank very high in Google Search engine results. Automated lead generating system and process for screening the tenant buyers.

- ✓ Access to the complete online Rent to Own course and materials conducted by my Coach and Mentor – Ross Lightle.

- ✓ Access to our Application Services at a substantial discount. This process will set your tenant buyers up for success and taps into our Power Team members, being our mortgage broker and credit coach.

✓ Access to our Contract Services at a substantial discount as well. You will always have the most up to date contracts filled in for each of your projects.

✓ Monthly live cast coaching session to help you grow your business.

✓ Your homeowners will receive videos from me trying to get them to take the next step, either to contact you for a consultation or to say YES to the lease option.

✓ Your tenant buyer prospects will receive videos to encourage them to take the next step and go through the application process. This will get them qualified for your Rent To Own program.

✓ I help you build your real estate investment business and you get to keep 100% of your leads and deals.

✓ You make money on any of the services we offer that are available to your homeowners or tenant buyers.

✓ Monthly Internet submissions targeted to both homeowners and tenant buyers to increase your visibility and exposure, as well as increase your search rank on Google and other search engines.

✓ Unlimited email access to me for support.

As a Certified Consultant you get to keep 100% of the lease option and sandwich lease option deals. My objective is simple and clear, do whatever I can to help grow your business, generate money and put you in a position where you can use the money you make in this business to live the life you have always dreamed. To ensure success for all our Certified Consultants they will be chosen by application process and limited for each city.

I've been helping businesses and real estate investors achieve their dreams for nearly a decade by creating systems, process and procedures using technology and marketing to make things streamlined and automated. I can help you, too.

To access the free information and to find out more about the various packages available, visit www.InfiniteRealEstateRoi.com to take advantage of all the resources included with this book.

To get FREE updates to this book, along with the accompanying videos, resources and materials referenced that will allow you to create your very own automated "SILVER BULLET" to help you control millions in real estate and generate a 6-figure yearly income

visit www.InfiniteRealEstateRoi.com

OR text your name and email to (587) 800-1551

OR Scan the QR Code

Chapter 11

THE FINE PRINT*

*the one our attorney wants us to share with you :(

The content, case studies and examples shared in this book do not in any way represent the "average" or "typical" member experience. In fact, as with any product or service, we know that some members purchase our systems and never use them, and therefore get no results from their membership whatsoever. You should assume that you will obtain no results with this program. Therefore, the member case studies we are sharing can neither represent nor guarantee the current or future experience of other past, current or future members. Rather, these member case studies represent what is possible with our system. Each of these unique case studies, and any and all results reported in these case studies by individual members, are the culmination of numerous variable, many of which we cannot control, including pricing, target market conditions, product/service quality, offer, customer service, personal initiative, and countless other tangible and intangible factors.

Whether this Notice refers to "you," "your," or "user," it means "you," while "we" or "our" refers to Rent To Own Revolution Inc.

Any earnings or income statements, or earnings income examples, are only estimates of what we think you could earn. There is no assurance you'll do as well. If you rely upon our figures, you must accept the risk of not doing as well.

Where specific income figures are used, and attributed to an individual or business, those persons or businesses have earned that amount. There is no assurance you'll do as well. If you rely upon our figures, you must accept the risk of not doing as well.

Moreover, where specific website traffic or search engine ranking results are used and attributed to an individual or business, those persons or businesses have achieved those results. There is no assurance you'll do as well. If you rely upon our figures, you must accept the risk of not doing as well.

Any and all claims or representations, regarding income earnings on www.InfiniteRealEstateROIBook.com, are not considered to be as average earnings. Likewise, any and all claims or representations, as to web site traffic or search engine ranking results on www.InfiniteRealEstateROIBook.com, are not to be considered as average results.

There can be no assurance that any prior successes, or past results, regarding income earnings, website traffic or search engine ranking results can be used as an indication of your future success or results.

Real Estate monetary and income results are based on many factors. We have no way of knowing how well you will do, as we do not know you, your background, your work ethic, or your business skills or practices. Therefore we do not guarantee or imply that you will get rich, that you will do as well, or make any money at all. There is no assurance you'll do as well. If you rely upon our figures, you must accept the risk of not doing as well.

Likewise, website traffic or search engine ranking results are based on many factors. We have no way of knowing how well you will do, as we do not know you, your background, your work ethic, or your business skills or practices. Therefore we do not guarantee or imply that you will get traffic, that you will do as well, or achieve website traffic or optimal search engine rankings at all. There is no assurance you'll do as well. If you reply upon your

John A. McCabe